IMAGES
of America

CATHEDRAL
CAVERNS

IMAGES
of America

CATHEDRAL CAVERNS

To John and Nancy,
All best,
[signature]

Whitney A. Snow

ARCADIA
PUBLISHING

Copyright © 2017 by Whitney A. Snow
ISBN 978-1-4671-2460-7
Ok,
Published by Arcadia Publishing
Charleston, South Carolina

Printed in the United States of America

Library of Congress Control Number: 2016945810

For all general information, please contact Arcadia Publishing:
Telephone 843-853-2070
Fax 843-853-0044
E-mail sales@arcadiapublishing.com
For customer service and orders:
Toll-Free 1-888-313-2665

Visit us on the Internet at www.arcadiapublishing.com

*For my mother, Barbara J. Snow, and in
memory of my father, Donald J. Snow*

CONTENTS

Acknowledgments   6

Introduction   7

1.   Jay Gurley's Exploration and Development of
      Cathedral Caverns   9

2.   People, Vistas, and Events at Cathedral Caverns   43

3.   Transition of Ownership and Formation of
      Cathedral Caverns State Park   93

ACKNOWLEDGMENTS

I would like to express my appreciation to those who assisted in the creation of this book. The majority of images were shared by Kathleen Bearden, Judy Engel, Kenneth Gurley, and Robin Kirkland. Unless otherwise noted, all images appear courtesy of the Gurley family collection. Others came from *Advertiser-Gleam* editor Anthony Campbell, Guntersville city clerk Betty McGowin Jones, Kennamer Cove Trading Post owner Cheryl Kennamer, Guntersville Museum director Julie Patton, Marshall County Legislative Office executive director Judy Miller, Cathedral Caverns State Park superintendent Lamar Pendergrass, Cathedral Caverns State Park tour guide Alex Prickett, retired Lake Guntersville State Park naturalist Linda Reynolds, and the Guntersville Historical Society. Research suggestions and photograph leads were provided by Marshall County Archives volunteers Billy Alexander, Margene Black, Rosemary Darnell, Keith Finley, Larry Smith, Dr. J.F. "Pete" Sparks Jr., Betty Taylor, and Macey Taylor—all local historians who have fueled my zeal to learn more about the rich past of Marshall County. Cathedral Caverns State Park facility operator Judy Holderfield provided insightful answers to myriad questions. State senator Clay Scofield (R-District 9) helped identify subjects in a contemporary image. Given that I knew virtually nothing about TIFF files or DPI at the start of this project, my colleague Dr. Gary Goldberg, professor of art at Midwestern State University, provided invaluable advice. Scottsboro High School chemistry teacher Kerry Townsend made editorial comments. A shout-out goes to Mississippi State University doctoral candidate Alyssa Warrick, whose Mammoth Cave National Park research sparked my interest in the history of caves. Arcadia title managers Caitrin Cunningham and Sarah Gottlieb gave steadfast encouragement. Last but not least, profound thanks go to my mother Barbara Snow, who, because I reside in Texas, agreed to help find and scan images. A bushel and a peck, Mom!

INTRODUCTION

Jacob Bonder Gurley, the man behind Cathedral Caverns, was born in Dyersburg, Tennessee, on January 1, 1923. The youngest of 18 children belonging to Andrew and Dora Gurley, he took a fancy to entertainment at a young age. Blessed with a vivid imagination, Gurley became a dreamer. Rather than catching the acting bug, he preferred making magic from behind a camera. After spending some time in Hollywood, Gurley moved to Huntsville, Alabama, with his wife and children. Once there, he worked as an industrial photographer at Redstone Arsenal. An explorer by nature, he loved caves and soon stumbled upon one that changed his life forever.

While Bat Cave had few visitors, usually teenagers who rarely ventured farther than the entrance, it did have an interesting history. Stephen Silas "Babe" Wright claimed that his great-grandfather Isom, along with his four brothers, came to the area from Kentucky. While his brothers returned to Kentucky, Isom remained, but the family lost track of him. When the family sent relatives to visit, they were shocked to find him living in the cave. Wright family legend holds that Isom claimed he never would have survived without help from Native Americans. In 1861, the cave was owned by Levi Guthrie. During the Civil War, the cave was targeted for saltpeter, but few facts exist regarding the amount mined. According to lore, troops fleeing their posts hid in the cave. By 1897, the cave had come under the ownership of Lewis Bowman. When Gurley came on the scene in 1952, the cave belonged to Gordon Wright. These owners had used the farmland but had never developed the cave.

After delving into Bat Cave with his pal Don Fulton, Gurley formulated a plan to make it his own. Unlike those who came before him, Gurley saw the cave as having great potential as a tourist attraction. He rushed home and pitched the idea to his wife, Helen. At first, she did not share his impulse to purchase the cave. After weighing the financial costs and risks, she gave her blessing, and the two began working to make his dream a reality. Although a *Reader's Digest* article later credited Helen with renaming the cave Cathedral Caverns, the idea really came from her husband.

Upon taking out a loan, the Gurleys bought Bat Cave and 80 acres. They then moved their trailer and three children—Kenneth, Judy, and Kathleen—to a location near the cave. Laborers were hired to cut trees and remove dirt, rocks, and boulders so as to make a tour path. In 1953, William L. Grafton agreed to become a partner in the project. His help greatly alleviated the financial strain, so much so that Gurley left his job at the arsenal. Gurley then moved his family, which now included another daughter, Robin, to the grounds of the cave.

The early years were full of hardships. Gurley endured ailments ranging from broken bones to pneumonia. The process of readying the cave for visitors took much longer than expected. The spring that ran through the cave damaged the first path so much that another had to be built. Despite these disappointments, Gurley never lost hope. In June 1955, having overcome many adversities, the Gurleys opened Cathedral Caverns to the public.

Cathedral Caverns quickly gained in popularity, and hundreds of tourists descended on the cave each week. Granted, many of the initial visitors were from Marshall County or Alabama in general, but patrons soon ranged from as far as Germany to Japan. Gurley, realizing the cave's contribution to state tourism, aided in the creation of the Scenic North Alabama Association. Using his camera skills and a creative flair, he promoted the cave with postcards, images, and advertisements. He mailed thousands of brochures and solicited interviews with newspapers, magazines, journals, news stations, and television programs. It was not long before he caught the attention of the film industry.

Actor Cornel Wilde selected Cathedral Caverns as the setting for his upcoming movie *Caves of Night*. He and his wife/costar, Jean Wallace, visited Marshall County in June 1959 and again in December. Wilde arranged for preliminary shots, selected backgrounds, and recruited extras. Local spirits ran high until word arrived that a screenwriter's strike had begun. Because the screenplay had yet to be completed, Wilde postponed filming. Though the movie was never made, the hype had been good for business.

The 1960s were extremely eventful for Cathedral Caverns. The decade included an article in *Reader's Digest*, a Gov. George Wallace Appreciation Dinner, and a tour by Don McCoy, executive director of Pres. Lyndon Johnson's tourism initiative Discover America. Many students from North Atlantic Treaty Organization (NATO) member nations patronized the cave when visiting nearby Huntsville, home of Redstone Arsenal. It was also declared a Cold War fallout shelter. Though these events contributed to publicity efforts, financial problems weighed on Gurley's mind.

During this difficult time, two boons took place. In June 1972, the US Travel Service listed Cathedral Caverns as one of the best caves in the country. Not too long after, in May 1973, the US Department of the Interior's National Landmark Trust chose Cathedral Caverns as a National Natural Landmark. While thrilled by these honors, Gurley found himself slipping further into debt. Due to nearby road construction, he decided the cave would only open during summers. Debt continued to worsen, and with much regret, Gurley sold Cathedral Caverns on March 17, 1974.

The new owner, contractor Dave Du'Chemin, announced that the cave would operate 12 months a year. He saw it as an ideal concert venue and began seeking musicians. He also used a boxcar as a large sign and, with the view to start a zoo, purchased two lions. These efforts failed to produce the expected profit, and bankruptcy proceedings took place. Huntsville fabric shop owner Tom German purchased the cave at auction on August 2, 1977.

Bluegrass Hoppers, Inc., of Scottsboro soon leased the cave from German and on November 8, 1980, reopened it as Cathedral Caverns Bluegrass Park. Open seven days a week, the park often hosted competitions between musical groups. Few if any profits were reaped, and before long, the park shut its doors. German ran the cave for a while and, in time, received a purchase offer from the State of Alabama.

Many Marshall County politicians, like state senator Hinton Mitchem (D-Albertville), state senator Loyd Coleman (D-Arab), and state representative Gordon Moon (D-Guntersville), had encouraged this procurement by the state. Mitchem and Coleman worked to get the legislature to reserve $750,000 for Cathedral Caverns. They planned for part of the money to be used for the purchase and the rest for renovations. Unfortunately, the men faced opposition from colleagues who thought the project too expensive. Other critics believed the money might be better spent on existing parks. This reserve, coupled with German's asking price of $750,000, delayed the transaction. In mid-July 1987, Alabama purchased the cave and 461 acres for $500,000. The state quickly set about making improvements, but progress was plagued by financial constraints. Gurley, who still lived near the cave, had been brought in as an advisor and intended to manage the gift shop. For decades, he had longed for the cave to become a national or state park and was very supportive of the state's effort. Sadly, he never got to see the grand opening.

Cathedral Caverns State Park opened on May 5, 2000, and while those present cheered, something, or rather someone was missing. Jay Gurley, the man who had made all of this possible, had died on April 30, 1996. Shortly before his death, he reflected on his first inspiration at Bat Cave: "It was one of those moments in a lifetime that compels you to take a drastic step into the unknown." He had done just that by successfully transforming a rural north Alabama cave into a world-class tourist attraction. His dream had become a reality.

One

JAY GURLEY'S EXPLORATION AND DEVELOPMENT OF CATHEDRAL CAVERNS

In July 1952, industrial photographer Jacob "Jay" Bonder Gurley (right) and journalist Don Fulton heard about Bat Cave, a large cave in the Grant, Alabama, area, and received directions from a local man, Luther Campbell. When the two reached the site, they almost failed to see the opening because it was concealed by trees and brush. After clearing limbs from the entrance, they ventured inside.

The son of Andrew and Dora Gurley, Jay Gurley, then 29, had only lived in Alabama a short time. He worked as a photographer at Huntsville's Redstone Arsenal and spent most of his free time seeking adventure. An avid spelunker with plenty of moxie, he enjoyed investigating caves, especially ones whose secrets had yet to be uncovered.

Jay Gurley is pictured next to a striking rock formation. Isom Wright's descendants claimed he once lived alongside Cherokees in Bat Cave. Over the years, the land containing the cave had several owners, including Levi Guthrie in 1861 and Lewis Bowman in 1897. The cave was mined for saltpeter during the Civil War and was rumored to have been a hideout for deserters. (Courtesy of Betty McGowin Jones.)

Upon taking the first few steps, Jay Gurley and Don Fulton noticed that a darkness, one unlike anything they had ever experienced, seemed to envelop them. Though the men had gas lanterns, they were unable to see much of anything. They sensed the chamber was exceptionally large and began crawling on their stomachs to avoid falling into a chasm. (Courtesy of Cheryl Kennamer.)

As the hours passed, Jay Gurley and Don Fulton expressed awe at the sight of stalagmites, red limestone, and what looked like a frozen waterfall. To prove their presence, both scratched their names and the date. They had not been the first, as they noticed the carved names of Abe Kennamer, Sarah Kennamer, and Gordon Wright.

Taking a moment to absorb the sights, the silence, and the sensations, Jay Gurley commented that the chamber resembled a cathedral. In a moment of epiphany, he said, "Look, finding this thing—just seeing it—is probably the most important thing we'll ever do. Somebody must build walkways so others can see it."

When a filthy, bedraggled Jay Gurley returned home that night, he enthusiastically regaled his wife, Helen, with what he had seen. He said, "We discovered a great cave today. . . . I think I'm going to buy it." Initially, Helen responded with innate skepticism. Purchasing the cave struck her as a foolhardy notion and an expensive one at that.

After all, Jay Gurley did not earn much money, and they, along with their children Kenneth, Judy, and Kathleen, were living in a trailer. Completely enthralled with the caverns, Jay remained adamant about owning the property, so Helen eventually consented. In order to buy the cave and 80 acres, he obtained a $400 loan by using their trailer and car as collateral. Jay later reflected, "I hocked everything I owned."

Expressing an optimistic fervor, Jay Gurley seemed almost a man possessed. Although onlookers may have thought his actions impulsive or bizarre, he refused to allow criticism to sway him. In his words, "It comes a man's time to do something special in the world . . . and a man's got to do it." Upon becoming the owner of Bat Cave, he renamed it Cathedral Caverns.

Jay Gurley (shown) spent several years in California, where he attended photography school. While working at movie studios in Hollywood, he had taken shots of celebrities. A voracious reader and devotee to music, he adored movies and, according to his daughter Robin Gurley, "was definitely a Clark Gable type." In an article for the *Huntsville Times*, Allen Rankin says, "Others eyed stars; Jay Gurley found his heaven under earth. The Gurleys have never had the luxuries considered essential by more conventional and less courageous people . . . but in striving together to make an easy path to a wondrous hole in a mountain's heart, they have acquired assets that cannot be measured in tangibles. The Gurleys' biggest finds have not been made in a cave at all, but in smaller, even more remarkable regions of inner space—inside themselves."

On May 3, 1954, Helen Gurley (shown), an extremely artistic teacher from Michigan, asked her husband to take her into the cave, and Jay, anxious to affirm the marvel of his discovery, complied. Journalist Allen Rankin writes, "Helen Gurley knew little about caves but plenty about husbands." Thoroughly amazed, she announced her support of his attempt to share Cathedral Caverns with the world. She was, in the words of son Kenneth, "the guiding spirit for my Dad." Indeed, Helen and Jay were inseparable and shared a love and friendship few couples ever achieve. According to Rankin, "The Gurleys have made thousands of trips into their mile or so of inner space, but they have never completely explored it. 'We never will,' says Jay. 'There will never be enough time . . . and we'll never really "see" all we find.'"

Shown are, from left to right, Kenneth, Judy, and Kathleen Gurley. Animals like crickets, crawfish, and bats could be seen in the cave. As to local wildlife in general, deer had been virtually hunted out, but opossums, raccoons, and foxes were prevalent. While rarely seen, snakes were common. In fact, Robin Gurley remembered her father killing an enormously fat six-foot rattler.

Helen Gurley often brought water to the workers. Lacking finances, she and her husband had to rely on their own two hands, volunteers like Luther Campbell, and some paid laborers. Pack mules were also essential. Every night after work at Redstone Arsenal, Jay Gurley tried to finish the gradual process of clearing the entrance.

Jay Gurley hired locals to help him ready the cave for commercialization. Pictured are, from left to right, Billy Bearden, Ben Click, Dude Franks, Bryce Click, Harold Edmonds, Billy Barnes, Gregory Clay, and unidentified. The boys, who seem to be having fun as they aid in the clearing of the cave, used crosscut saws and likely brought their own axes. They also removed rocks, boulders, and dirt from the cave. (Courtesy of Cheryl Kennamer.)

Five teenagers are shown taking a break from rock removal. Their task was of utmost importance because Jay Gurley knew that to have a successful tour, the cave needed a path. The work was extremely labor-intensive and needed supplementation by blasting. These young men probably never imagined they were helping to create a state treasure.

Nannie and Luther Campbell

Luther Campbell is shown here with his wife, Nannie. They became surrogate grandparents to the Gurley children. During the first years, many incidents befell Jay Gurley. He broke an ankle, hit himself with a sledgehammer, snapped his Achilles heel, developed pneumonia, and had several hernias. Many men might have given up and cut their losses, but Jay stayed the course. (Courtesy of Cheryl Kennamer.)

In 1953, Jay Gurley partnered with William Grafton, a Redstone Arsenal executive engineer who expressed interest in the cave. With Grafton's financial backing, Gurley daringly resigned from his day job and moved his family, now comprised of six members given the birth of daughter Robin, down the road from the cave. This transition was eased by Marshall County's agreement to create a road connecting the cave to the highway.

In 1954, the cave's creek, named Mystery River because it was often heard and only occasionally seen, flooded, destroying the new path. Jay Gurley (shown) had cleared about 1,000 feet, so the loss of the trail was a monumental setback. Crestfallen, he expressed doubts, but his wife provided constant reassurance. When Robin Gurley was two, the family moved to the cave site. Remaking the cave was not for the faint of heart, and Jay was anything but. He sallied forth, refusing to rest until the job was done. According to an article in the *Atlanta Journal and Constitution Magazine*, "More than 6,000 wheelbarrow loads of rock were taken from the tunnel, and this was crushed and used on the trails." In a way, Jay was attempting to conquer or at least tame inner earth, and though the pace was slow, he was winning.

On his first impression of the pre-cleared cave, Kenneth Gurley said, "It was quite spectacular . . . something that you'd always remember. You're in the middle of some very dense woods, almost jungle-like and all of a sudden the woods stop and, what-in-the-world, you feel this cool blast of air coming at you. Then you look up and you realize you're standing in the mouth of the cave."

Jay Gurley immediately started building another path and hired John Vinson, a former Tennessee miner, to lay the needed dynamite. Every time Vinson prepared an explosion, one laborer always panicked and fled. Fortunately, there were never any related injuries. A path of stone was eventually completed. (Courtesy of Cheryl Kennamer.)

As word of the "caveman" and "one-man army" near Guntersville spread, Jay Gurley became the target of journalists. One article, "Door to Alabama Underground," which appears in the *Birmingham News Magazine*, speaks of the progress he had made in readying the cave for tourists. Its author, Roger Thames, describes the cave's entrance as "almost perfectly arched as if a man had built it."

Jay Gurley devoted himself to creating the necessary light, a difficult chore given the cave's vast darkness. Thames emphasized Gurley's skill with a camera and wrote of stalagmites, stalactites, and Mystery River, which, it turned out, ran through another cave before emerging at Bryant Spring in a valley near Gunter Mountain.

Thames equates the tour to "walking inside a rubber ball where the silence is deafening." Injecting a bit of macabre levity, he jokes that all the while, he kept thinking of "The Fate of Floyd Collins," a song about a cave-in victim who died before rescuers reached him. Thames survived unscathed.

Guntersville, the seat of Marshall County, Alabama, claimed Cathedral Caverns even though it was technically located in Woodville. Its newspaper, the *Advertiser-Gleam*, bestowed a great deal of publicity on a regular basis. One article, titled "World's Most Spectacular Caverns," tells of Gurley's goals as well as his discovery of fossils, Native American artifacts, and beautiful amethysts.

When Cathedral Caverns finally opened to the public in June 1955, people came from far and wide. One *Advertiser-Gleam* article bragged that in two months, the cave was visited each week by roughly 300 cars full of tourists. Impressed patrons could tell Jay Gurley had poured his lifeblood into the cave.

The newspaper informed readers of all the difficult acts Jay Gurley, shown here with a poster advertising an article about Cathedral Caverns in the *Reader's Digest*, had performed to prepare the cave for the public. This may have been in response to Gurley's shock at one tourist's statement: "Isn't it handy how this tunnel is just the right height all the way to walk through without bumping your head."

While heading a publicity campaign, Jay Gurley helped found the Scenic North Alabama Association in 1956 and was elected its president. The association included Ave Maria Grotto (Cullman); Citadel Rock (Fort Payne); Dismal Gardens (Russellville); Natural Bridge (Haleyville); Rickwood Caverns (Warrior); and Ivy Green (Tuscumbia). Guntersville Caverns eventually joined.

Although photographic sessions usually took hours, Jay Gurley believed it was time well spent. The resultant images were used in postcards and promotions. Something of a lay engineer, Gurley was constantly drafting plans. As his daughter Robin Gurley put it, "He would have all those plans drawn up and then he'd show up the next day, and he'd have it all worked out. And it would work."

Taking photographs in the cave was easier said than done. The bulbs along the walkway failed to provide enough light, so Jay Gurley had to improvise and exercise his creativity. He took flashbulbs and placed aluminum pie plates behind each to help reflect the light. When they were fired all at once, color photographs were produced.

This is an image of the entrance prior to its being cleared. Given that it was inevitably the first thing tourists noticed, Jay Gurley strove to make it inviting. Finding a median between too many trees and too few was challenging. Beckoning onlookers to enter, the opening attracted visitors with its beauty, mystery, and historical significance.

In August 1955, after the cave had been open a month, the *Advertiser-Gleam* offered helpful hints to those touring the site. Titled "Bring a Wrap," the piece advises visitors to wear warm clothing, namely sweaters. The prime tourist season was, of course, summer, so most patrons simply wore short sleeves and shorts or skirts.

The cave entrance looks especially ominous during winter. This huge maw provided a chance to escape blistering heat in spring and summer and, in winter, an opportunity to flee from the cold. When temperatures reached over 100 degrees Fahrenheit or dropped below freezing, the cave stayed a temperate 60 degrees. (Courtesy of Cheryl Kennamer.)

In March 1957, Jay Gurley started taking color photographs of Goliath, a gigantic column 243 feet wide and 45 feet tall. This image shows Clifford Gamble standing atop a rock at the base of Goliath. Gurley removed these boulders so tourists could get close and admire the size of this formation. Goliath quickly became the most popular feature in the cave. (Courtesy of Cheryl Kennamer.)

An amateur archaeologist, Edward C. Mahan, shown here in 1957, devoted his evenings, weekends, and holidays to excavation. The University of Alabama provided gasoline money to Mahan and Dr. A.G. Long, a Guntersville optometrist, in exchange for their finding dig sites for its students. One of Mahan's favorite locations was Cathedral Caverns.

The Alabama Archeological Society's journal *Stones and Bones* devoted an entire page to Edward Mahan (pictured), A.G. Long, and Jerry Long when they began seeking artifacts and skeletal remains inside Cathedral Caverns. During their digs, the explorers found tools, weapons, cooking utensils, and animal bones. They had hoped to uncover human remains, but much to their disappointment, none were ever found.

Mahan dug pits about eight feet deep and discovered many artifacts, especially arrowheads and spear points. In Mahan's words, "We found plenty of his [Native Americans] tools in Madison County but never have been able to tie him to a certain spot. This cave is a logical habitat. I think we will find indisputable evidence that he once lived here."

Edward Mahan (far left) and his Redstone Arsenal spelunking buddies, including Jim Maloney (second from left), are shown in nearby Guffey Cave. Bear bones, gauged by the Smithsonian Institution to be anywhere from 10,000 to 40,000 years old, were found there. The bones were actually discovered by Redstone Arsenal troops who sought Mahan's council. He then led an excavation in that cave.

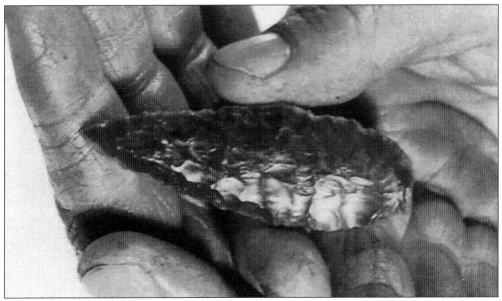

This artifact, found at Cathedral Caverns, is at the Smithsonian Institution. Jay Gurley liked collecting arrowheads and looked for them not only at Cathedral Caverns but also in area farm fields. He, like Edward Mahan, appreciated the magnitude of the cave's contribution to Native American history. Mahan loaned him a Native American canoe to display at the caverns.

Shown is Dr. A.G. Long. Edward Mahan had discovered the canoe in an embankment at Madison County's Hobbs Island. The find was a thrill, and Mahan sought to find a way to share his discovery. Cathedral Caverns, given its former Native American presence, seemed an ideal home for the canoe. Jay Gurley prized this addition to the cave, but the canoe disappeared shortly after the cave came under new ownership in the 1970s. (Courtesy of Marshall County Archives.)

Edward Mahan, who lived in the Honeycomb community, worked at Redstone Arsenal until he retired around 1970. Passionate about archaeology, he helped form the Alabama Archaeological Society as well as the Huntsville and Marshall County chapters. Published in the *Journal of Alabama Archaeology* and *Anthropological Journal of Canada* among others, he pursued his archaeology hobby until his June 1984 death in the Point of Pines community near Warrenton.

In 1974, the State of Alabama and the Huntsville Speleological Society mapped Cathedral Caverns. The tour path was 3,588 feet; the highest point was 760 feet; and the lowest place was 656 feet. Near Goliath, the width was 152 feet. Between March and December 1993, a cartography project mapped 11,012 feet.

Several archaeological digs, both amateur and educational, were conducted at Cathedral Caverns over the years. In the late 1980s, Dr. Danny Vaughn from Jacksonville State University studied the cave. Another consortium from the University of Alabama, Jacksonville State, and Northeast Alabama Community College organized to unearth artifacts in 1988. Finding evidence of charcoal remains amazed the researchers.

After unearthing charcoal, University of Alabama archaeologist Dr. Carey Oakley, who co-led the dig with Jacksonville State University professor Harry Holstein, said, "I'm convinced man was in Alabama 12,000 years ago." However, the deeper the dig went, the fewer artifacts were found. The experts theorized that Cathedral Caverns was not a permanent dwelling. Instead, it perhaps served as the equivalent of a vacation home or a religious retreat.

Edward Mahan is shown. The consortium found mussel shells. Since the cave is about 20 miles from the Tennessee River, man had to have taken the mussels to the site. This distance partially explained why the caverns never served as a permanent dwelling. Harry Holstein stated, "In modern-day terms, you might say we found things like you might take on a picnic, not the good china you keep at home."

Pictured is Edward Mahan. While the consortium only dug roughly four feet below the cave floor, they uncovered some artifacts dating back at least 8,000 years. The bulk of what they found, however, was 3,000 years old. According to one volunteer, Van King, "We've been finding little fragments of earlier stuff mixed with it." One flint drill was thought to be one of the oldest artifacts ever found in Alabama.

This a grindstone found in Cathedral Caverns. While bones of bears, deer, opossums, and bats were discovered, no human remains were located. It has been suggested that Native Americans may have associated the cave with the supernatural and, for whatever reason, did not choose to bury their dead there. (Courtesy of Linda Reynolds.)

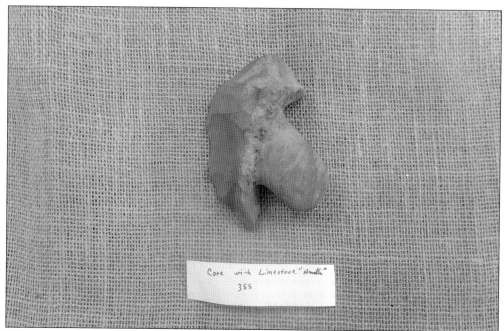

This is a core with a limestone "handle." Carey Oakley and Harry Holstein welcomed volunteers, and Guntersville Girl Scout leader Jean Ann Moon brought her troop to help sift for bones, pottery shards, and arrowheads. The girls, among whom were Michelle Ortega-Edwards, Poppy Moon, Kelly Quinn, and Jessica Krichev, really enjoyed the experience. (Courtesy of Linda Reynolds.)

A conch shell was thought to have been a drinking cup. Of the twenty-one students who participated in the consortium dig, nine were from Jacksonville State University, eleven were from Northeast Alabama Community College, and one came from the University of Alabama. During the excavation, the professors stayed in a Guntersville hotel, and the students resided near the cave entrance. (Courtesy of Linda Reynolds.)

The description on this artifact reads as follows: "A fine white powder found in the test pit. This was used for war paint, when mixed with bear grease. It was also used in the making of pottery." Among the Jacksonville State students were Lee Pierce and Tex Williams. All the while, Jay Gurley lent the dig an eager hand. (Courtesy of Linda Reynolds.)

These are limestone hoe fragments. According to an article in the *Advertiser-Gleam*, "Dr. Oakley said the key to tracing ancient history is finding tools, bones, pottery, etc. still buried in the earth where they can be dated. An arrowhead or spear point that's found in a field after a bulldozer or plow unearths it is interesting, but not a lot of help to scientists." (Courtesy of Linda Reynolds.)

These are preforms made from agate and chalcedony. The Marshall County chapter of the Alabama Archaeological Society formed in November 1960. Its charter officers were as follows: A.G. Long (Guntersville), president; E.C. Mahan (Honeycomb), vice president; Jay Gurley (Woodville), secretary-treasurer; and Leon Kennamer (Guntersville), publicity chairman. (Courtesy of Linda Reynolds.)

Shown is a mineral formation in Cathedral Caverns. Charter members of the Marshall County chapter of the Alabama Archaeological Society included Acton Boone, Claude Herbert Smith, John Brookshire, Ed Neely, Eugene Hatcher, and Roscoe Bynum. The chapter planned to "promote the study of archaeology in Alabama . . . keep records . . . and preserve important archaeological sites."

Shown from left to right are 1959 Marshall County High School freshmen Barbara Smith, Richie Starnes, Brenda Brown, and Buddy Scruggs. Many cave artifacts were displayed in the gift shop or kept as Gurley family treasures. Kenneth Gurley's favorite was an effigy pipe. According to Robin Gurley, there was once a Native American mound at the cave entrance, but it was leveled when Cathedral Caverns came under new ownership. (Courtesy of Barbara Snow.)

Bill Grafton is shown leading a tour. *Stones and Bones*, a public television show that aired out of Birmingham, requested two interviews with Jay Gurley in 1958. In February, Gurley remarked on the archaeological value of Cathedral Caverns. That April, he spoke of the cave's rich history and his goal to make it a state and perhaps even nationally known tourist destination.

Joe and Gwen Reeves excavated and opened Guntersville Caverns off Highway 79 on June 15, 1958. The second underground attraction for Marshall County advertised level parking areas, sanded walkways, a concession stand, and lighting designed by the Tennessee Valley Authority (TVA). Formerly known as Salt Petre Cave, the caverns conducted business until roughly the early 1970s. (Courtesy of Guntersville Museum.)

The first guides for Guntersville Caverns were Wayne Mosley, Gordon Cowen Jr., and Buddy Duvall. While conducting tours, they enthralled groups with funny names like "Old King Cole's Knee Bones" and "Whosababies" for sandstone formations that resembled people and animals. More seriously, they claimed one structure favored a biblical scene of Joseph and Mary. (Courtesy of Guntersville Museum.)

"Whosababy" Formations
GUNTERSVILLE CAVERNS

The Guntersville Caverns had excavated sea fossils and a host of archaeological items. Carl Miller from the Smithsonian Institution authenticated the artifacts. A chipping site used by Native Americans was found. The Reeves' advertisements proclaimed 10,000-year-old driftwood and fossilized fish from the time the area was at the bottom of a sea. (Courtesy of Guntersville Museum.)

Helen and Robin Gurley are shown on Easter Sunday. When she was about five, Robin had a memorable Halloween. Her mother dressed her as a ghost and took her into the cave where "they [her siblings] would jump out at different points and try to scare me, talk to me, and give me treats. How neat. How fun. It was so special."

For Robin Gurley, shown between her parents, the concession shop, with its spears, drums, headdresses, and teacups, not to mention candy and colas, was "paradise to me as a kid." She also loved playing with the kittens her mother sometimes kept in a box near the counter. As Robin laughed, "I can tell you there were a couple of times when kittens went home with some kids."

Pictured are, from left to right, Marshall County High School eighth graders Chippy Manning, John Brown, Judy Starnes, Cynthia Burk, and Mary Catherine Coplin in 1959. Robin Gurley enjoyed pretending to be a Native American princess, looking for tadpoles, and exploring the woods. Her favorite place was a ring of limestone rock above the cave entrance. She spent hours there playing house and watching tourists. (Courtesy of Barbara Snow.)

Shown from left to right are 1959 Marshall County High School sophomores Frankie McClendon, Brenda Wray, Nancy Smith, and Larry Whitaker. At 12, Robin Gurley started a side business: "Somebody told Dad that carrying a buckeye in your pocket was good luck. So he told me 'There's your business. Pick up buckeyes, wash 'em up, and put 'em out on the counter. 5 cents apiece.' So that's what I did." (Courtesy of Barbara Snow.)

Kathleen, Robin, Judy, and Kenneth Gurley all contributed to the family business. Kenneth, for one, gave about six tours a day. On one occasion, the cave began to flood. Heroically, he led 30 tourists through waist-deep water back to the entrance. Another time, he fell 30–40 feet while rappelling. While waiting for his friends to rescue him, he found another chamber, which extended the tour by a quarter of a mile.

Once a tour group had walked about 500 feet, the guide said, "This area in a cave or caverns is called the twilight zone. This is where daylight ends and darkness begins." Total darkness, when guides switched off the lights, was very popular. In that pitch-black minute, some, eager for any speck of light, may have exhibited fear, while others deemed the experience exhilarating. (Courtesy of Cathedral Caverns State Park.)

Jay Gurley is shown posing with Mary Ellen Morrow. During the tours, Jay typically instructed his guides to put out the lights in the Stalagmite Forest. His guide script reads, "This is total darkness. If you can see your hand well, you have a good imagination. Once lost in this darkness, it would be impossible to find the way out." (Courtesy of *Advertiser-Gleam*.)

Two

PEOPLE, VISTAS, AND EVENTS AT CATHEDRAL CAVERNS

This is a contraption meant to better facilitate tours. Pictured are, from left to right, (seated) Robin Gurley, Jackie Hodges, Ray Selvage, Jimmy Cooper, and Walter Wright; (standing) Jay Gurley, Helen Gurley, Barry Colburn, Larry Colburn, Milton Franks, and Joe Dabbs. Each year, Jay chose a color theme, and in this photograph, the guides are wearing orange blazers.

This is the original Cathedral Caverns Welcome Center, which included both concessions and souvenirs. When it was eventually replaced, Robin Gurley kept a treasured piece of the building's wood, but it has since disappeared. Observe that Jay Gurley had taken great pains to place rocks along the sides of the nearby stream.

Jay Gurley drove his snow-covered car to the base of Goliath to highlight its size and escape the freezing weather. In the hopes that this photograph might be used in automobile advertisements, he sent it to several dealerships, but unfortunately, nothing came of the effort. This is yet another example of how he constantly brainstormed about how to publicize the cave.

Shown clockwise from right are Kenneth, Robin, Judy, and Kathleen Gurley. After adding a living room, a master bedroom, and a laundry/bathroom to the trailer, Jay Gurley also built a stereo system from scratch. He put the speakers on the porch, aimed them at the cave, and played both classical music and show tunes. Music was always present during the fish fries he hosted for friends and family.

Pictured from left to right are Grant locals Delphine Wright, Fay Bishop, Edith Perkins, and Mary Ellen Campbell. Even when Campbell married and moved to Kansas City, Missouri, she wrote Jay Gurley letters emphasizing that not even Carlsbad Caverns could compare with Cathedral Caverns. Such words of faith gave him much-needed encouragement.

Jay Gurley called Goliath "the world's largest stalagmite," but given that it spanned from ground to ceiling, this description was technically incorrect. Stalagmites emerge from the ground, unlike stalactites, which emerge from the ceiling. Neither connects from floor to ceiling. Gurley believed a column, Goliath, cemented his cave as "The Greatest Show in Earth."

There were rumors that the cave was haunted by Native Americans, Confederate soldiers, and even extraterrestrials. Some claimed to have seen glowing orbs levitating throughout the chambers. The "Curse of Cathedral Caverns" was especially discussed after one failed movie at the site and another that almost ended in tragedy.

Jay Gurley's partner, Bill Grafton, seen with a group in the top right corner, sometimes led tours. Gurley called the new walkway, completed at 276 feet by later summer 1958, "the really spectacular part of the caverns." It allowed spectators to see not merely the canyon in what he called the "world's largest cave room" but also the frozen waterfall beyond. (Courtesy of Cheryl Kennamer.)

Bill Grafton is shown guiding a tour through Big Rock Canyon. During the summer of 1958, tourism rose 20 percent as Cathedral Caverns made nationwide headlines. One journalist for the *Greenville Delta Democrat Times* wrote that she and her family planned to drive through the Tennessee Valley and stop by Cathedral Caverns, "whose natural entrance is said to be one of the largest in the world." (Courtesy of Cheryl Kennamer.)

ONE OF THE GIANT COLUMNS IN THE

STALAGMITE FOREST IN

CATHEDRAL CAVERNS, GRANT, ALABAMA

"WORLD'S GREATEST CAVERN DISCOVERY"

A promotional photograph of the Stalagmite Forest shows Robin Gurley sitting on the front of the jeep and Ross and June Graves in the front seat. While many tourists were hesitant about the cave, Robin said, "I would go on tours and even now when I go on tours and they get to the point where its farthest underground, people get a little apprehensive. And the total darkness thing, since I'd been in there so much, that didn't bother me. After I got a bit older and I would get to the point where it ends and even now, I would picture in my mind how to get back out. If there were no lights at all ever. And I think I could have done it." In her words, "When I go to the cave and as I walk down toward the entrance and smell that earthy, cool air, I'm home."

Grant boys, including Raymond Farr (center), hauled sand from the end of the commercial tour in order to build trails throughout the caverns. In addition to wheelbarrows, washtubs, as seen in the background, were used to transport sand. While the work was difficult, the laborers saw it as an adventure and a once-in-a-lifetime experience.

Kenneth Gurley is pictured. Jay Gurley dubbed this formation, three inches wide and almost 30 feet high, "the world's most improbable stalagmite." He argued that Cathedral Caverns could rightly lay claim to the title of "World's No. 1 Cavern" because it had the "world's largest entrance, cave room, stalagmite, frozen waterfall, flowstone wall, stalagmite forest, underground canyon, and the most improbable stalagmite." (Courtesy of Betty McGowin Jones.)

Gov. James E. "Big Jim" (left) and First Lady Jamelle Folsom (second from left) appeared at the Guntersville Chamber of Commerce in January 1958. That year, Cathedral Caverns received an increase in guests. Visitors logged ranged from Alaska and Nebraska to Belgium, France, and Germany. Local and state officials took notice and scrambled to promote the cave, Lake Guntersville, and other area sights. (Courtesy of Jerry W. Cornelius Collection, Guntersville Historical Society.)

In January 1959, the *Advertiser-Gleam* reported that the movie *Caves of Night* might be filmed at Cathedral Caverns. Based on John Carpenter's 1958 novel *The Caves of Night*, the Columbia Pictures flick was set to star Cornel Wilde; his wife, Jean Wallace; Cliff Robertson; Diane Foster; and Glenn Corbett. (Courtesy of Jerry W. Cornelius Collection, Guntersville Historical Society.)

This column reaches over 50 feet in height. Cathedral Caverns had everything star and producer Cornel Wilde wanted: "Big forest of rock formations, a big underground room, an underground stream subject to flooding, and a surrounding countryside with mountains, lakes, and lakeside cottages." Mystery River may not have been as high as he desired, but he figured it could be dammed. (Courtesy of Betty McGowin Jones.)

Guntersville buzzed with excitement at the prospect of celebrities descending on the area. Local motels eagerly offered to house the stars, technicians, artists, photographers, and anyone else affiliated with the movie. While many volunteered to become extras, Columbia Pictures remained unconvinced that Guntersville was the ideal setting. (Courtesy of Guntersville Museum.)

CATHEDRAL CAVERNS

KENNAMER'S COVE

Woodville   Alabama   Grant

Cornel Wilde had never heard of Cathedral Caverns until contacted by Bill Grafton. While on a business trip in California, Grafton learned that Wilde was searching for a cave site. Intrigued, Wilde soon narrowed his options to Cathedral Caverns and one other unspoken possibility. In the end, Wilde chose Cathedral Caverns. Columbia Pictures, however, wanted three guarantees. (Courtesy of Guntersville Museum.)

Shown is Robin Gurley. Columbia Pictures required assurances from the city of Guntersville and Wilde. First, the community had to recruit and provide extras who would work for free and provide their own costumes. Second, locals were expected to decorate sets without pay. Third, the movie was supposed to be set in Austria, so the studio wanted fields of flowers.

In preparation for filming, Cornel Wilde and Jean Wallace visited Guntersville twice. Among the locals they befriended were the McGowins, owners of the Lake Shore Motel, and the Hembrees, owners of a Buick dealership. From left to right are (first row) Jean Wallace, Helen Gurley, and Giselle Hembree; (second row) John Bains, Clifford McGowin, Cornel Wilde, and Bob Hembree. Wilde, who often played strong men with a sweet or comical side, had always been a popular leading man. His acting style, though seen by some as a bit stagey, seemed best suited to roles in which he starred opposite a feisty leading lady like Maureen O'Hara in *At Sword's Point* (1952), Yvonne De Carlo in *Passion* (1954), or Jane Russell in *Hot Blood* (1956). Wilde's wife was a much more subdued actress whose skills were best exhibited in dramas. (Courtesy of Betty McGowin Jones.)

Fantastic Forest

This image was taken by Huntsville photographer Ernest McMeans. Leon Kennamer, a local professional photographer, and Dr. Jake Long were hired to make preliminary photographs and identify possible set locations in Cathedral Caverns. All told, it took them, with the help of the film's art director Cary O'Dell, about 11 hours. Firing 250 bulbs, the group shot 65 photographs. (Courtesy of Cheryl Kennamer.)

The Marshall County High School Band is shown on parade in the late 1950s. The entire Gurley family thoroughly liked Cornel Wilde and Jean Wallace. In the words of Robin Gurley, "They were very nice people. No pretension at all. They seemed to mix in when we had dinners. They just fit right in. They were beautiful people. Very down to Earth." (Courtesy of the Jerry W. Cornelius Collection, Guntersville Historical Society.)

Bill Grafton and the Gurleys met Cornel Wilde and Jean Wallace at the Huntsville Airport in June. While in Guntersville, the stars resided with Clifford and Virginia McGowin at the Lake Shore Courts. A facsimile of the residence still exists (shown) and is owned by Warren Jones, son of Junior and Betty McGowin Jones. (Author's collection.)

During this visit to Guntersville, Cornel Wilde dined with a city commissioner and received personal tours of the caverns from Jay Gurley. Spellbound by the spacious chambers and enormous stalagmites, Wilde set about selecting filming locations. Basking in the charming scenery and "southern hospitality," he and his wife expressed delight at having found such a promising site. (Courtesy of Betty McGowin Jones.)

While in town, Cornel Wilde (right) and Jean Wallace stayed with Aredell McGowin, the mother of Clifford McGowin (left). When Wallace asked to wash one of Wilde's shirts in the sink, Clifford's wife Virginia (center) agreed and, seeking bragging rights, asked if she might have the privilege of ringing out a star's garment. (Courtesy of Betty McGowin Jones.)

Jean Wallace could often be seen relaxing outside of the Lake Shore Motel. During a December trip to Guntersville, she used Harris Laundry, received a manicure at La Verne's Beauty Shop, and visited a Girl Scout troop in Claysville. While those who met her felt obliged to say "Miss Wallace" or "Mrs. Wilde," she said, "Call me Jean." It was this informality that made locals love her all the more. (Courtesy of Betty McGowin Jones.)

Kenneth and Judy Gurley (right) enjoyed visiting with Jean Wallace in the welcome center. Helen described the celebrities as follows: "They are just the nicest, friendliest folks you ever met. They were very much interested in everything about the area and had more to talk about than we had time." Asked if autograph requests bothered him, Cornel Wilde said, "Not a bit." (Courtesy of Betty McGowin Jones.)

Robin (center) and Kathleen (right) Gurley were equally thrilled to meet the glamorous but down-to-earth Jean Wallace. Their friend Betty McGowin remembered her as being sweet, beautiful, and fun. Wallace had a ritual of brushing her hair so many strokes before bed. One night, she paid Judy McGowin a dollar to brush her hair, and the little girl treasured the memory. (Courtesy of Betty McGowin Jones.)

Judy McGowin is shown posing for a photograph in Cathedral Caverns. The *Advertiser-Gleam* claimed Cornel Wilde had gone from *"The Greatest Show on Earth* [1952] to the Greatest Show in Earth." This referenced one of Wilde's more famous roles as acrobatic wonder the Great Sebastian—which seems rather odd since Wilde admitted to having acrophobia. (Courtesy of Betty McGowin Jones.)

While Cornel Wilde explored Cathedral Caverns, Jean Wallace spent most of her time with the McGowins. She turned many a head in a bathing suit, especially when she accepted Clifford McGowin's offer to give her water-skiing lessons. Lake Guntersville had, by that time, become a popular tourist attraction, and Wallace fell under its spell. (Courtesy of Betty McGowin Jones.)

This is an image of Bill Grafton leading a tour. Locals had a field day when their beloved city was catapulted into national headlines. From the *Cleveland Plain Dealer* to the *San Diego Union*, newspapers talked of Guntersville and its Hollywood connection. While enthusiasm soared throughout Marshall County, Columbia Pictures continued to have a number of concerns. (Courtesy of Betty McGowin Jones.)

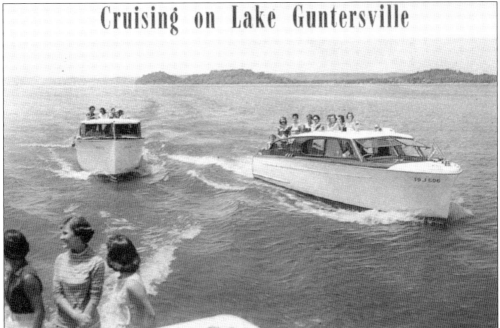

The movie studio fretted that Guntersville could not provide enough extras. The Guntersville Chamber of Commerce recruited heavily, and tryouts were held by Clifford McGowin, Lyle Wilkins, and Claude Hendon. To boost interest, the *Advertiser-Gleam* printed that prizes would be given to extras with the best costumes. (Courtesy of Jerry W. Cornelius Collection, Guntersville Historical Society.)

Ray Selvage is shown leading a tour. Those interested in becoming extras were asked to submit a slip, printed in the *Advertiser-Gleam*, to either the Guntersville Chamber of Commerce or the Lake Theater. By Christmas, only 16 people had completed these applications. Since participation was minimal, Cornel Wilde nixed the festival scene on Lake Guntersville. (Courtesy of Guntersville Museum.)

This is a rare glimpse of Jay Gurley (right) without his signature mustache. During the December trip, Cornel Wilde (center, facing camera) patronized many Guntersville establishments like LaPere's Coffee Shop. He and his wife dined on quail at the home of the Hembrees. While most wanted to defer and call him "Mr. Wilde," the leading man insisted that they call him Cornel. At one point, he even tried a batch of local moonshine.

Lake Theater owner Bill Harris wanted the movie's premiere to be in Guntersville. When asked, Cornel Wilde said, "I'd like to see it held here." However, he explained that the studio usually held openings "where they can get the biggest splash of publicity." The choice of setting was never decided because the movie was never made. (Courtesy of Jerry W. Cornelius Collection, Guntersville Historical Society.)

Kate Duncan Smith DAR High School students are shown at the cave in 1955. Due to a screenwriters' strike, Cornel Wilde delayed the movie. When the strike ended, interest in the project had vanished, and *Caves of Night* remained an unrealized dream for Wilde, Jay Gurley, and the people of Marshall County, especially those in Guntersville. (Courtesy of Guntersville Museum.)

Judy Gurley is shown behind the desk in the gift shop. In a letter to Jay Gurley, Cornel Wilde writes, "I am very sorry . . . and all the work spent by all of us on it so far to get things ready and then to be stalled . . . plans in the future . . . depend . . . on the nature of the market, and what sort of cast will be available when we return."

Jay (far right) and Helen (second from left) Gurley savored their time with Cornel Wilde and Jean Wallace. While the strike put filming on a permanent hiatus, they tried to view the experience in a positive light. It had afforded them scads of free publicity (including mentions on television shows like *Masquerade Party* and plugs in the columns of Hedda Hopper and Louella Parsons), and more importantly, they had made wonderful memories.

The 1961 Marshall County High School's yearbook, *The Marshall*, includes shots of freshman class officers, from left to right, Ann Segers, Pete Sparks, Ann Lee, and Dale Collins inside Cathedral Caverns. Photographer Leon Kennamer selected the backdrops. The cave was also a popular setting for photographs of students from other area schools, like Kate Duncan Smith DAR High School and Scottsboro High School. (Courtesy of Barbara Snow.)

Marshall County High School sophomore officers, from left to right, Joe Starnes, Judy Starnes, Milla McCord, and Richard Sparks also posed in Cathedral Caverns. Including these scenes as part of the yearbook, *The Marshall*, provided lovely scenery while advertising the caverns to locals. Seeing the smiles on the faces of the students probably incited more than a few onlookers to get in on the fun and tour the cave. (Courtesy of Barbara Snow.)

Shown from left to right are Dickie Mason, Johnnie Smith, Bill Jones, and Buddy Scruggs, all junior officers at Marshall County High School. Rather than use stock pictures as divider pages, *The Marshall* staff opted to try something different. The yearbook staff hoped to add a touch of local history by capturing scenes at the area's world-class attraction— Cathedral Caverns. (Courtesy of Barbara Snow.)

Yearbook photographs like this one of Marshall County High School senior officers, from left to right, Mary Carlton, Ben Harrison, Don Ryan, Bobby Smith, and Skip Norrell placed glimpses of Cathedral Caverns in the hands of families in the high school's service area. Jay Gurley welcomed those who wanted to use the cave as a background. In modern terms, he was an advocate of staycations. (Courtesy of Barbara Snow.)

The culmination of this session was a photograph of all of the Marshall County High School officers in the cave's last chamber. Jay Gurley received mail through Woodville but also had a post office box in Grant. While a Marshall County cave, Cathedral Caverns, due to its proximity to Madison County and especially Jackson County, was prized by many other cities. (Courtesy of Barbara Snow.)

A group of students from Jackson County's Scottsboro High School wore costumes when they were photographed by a professional photographer in Cathedral Caverns. Such photo shoots typically lasted at least 30 minutes. Jay Gurley relished seeing how the cave fueled the imaginations of children and teenagers. This is one of many cavemen-themed photographs.

On September 27, 1965, the Grant Jaycees and Jaycettes hosted a George Wallace Appreciation Dinner in the entrance of Cathedral Caverns. Although the catered, formal event was difficult to organize, the dinner was a smashing success. Jay Gurley took great pains to provide substantial lighting, and the end result provided lovely ambiance.

At the $6-a-plate affair, the master of ceremonies was local tax assessor Ray McClendon. George Wallace (pictured) was introduced by Bill Jones Jr., originally from Woodville, who once served as the governor's press secretary. Jones called Wallace "Alabama's greatest governor." This sentiment was echoed by Jaycee president Clifford Gamble, an employee at the caverns.

At the dinner, Gov. George C. Wallace (left) was recognized for his myriad efforts to help Marshall County. Given the county's reliance on tourism, locals valued Wallace's contributions in advertising "Alabama the Beautiful." His first wife, Lurleen, who later became Alabama's first and only woman governor, also shared a devotion to promoting the state. Though many saw her election as nothing more than a continuation of George, who had been unable to seek reelection due to term limitations at that time, Lurleen had a mind of her own and took her position very seriously. Marshall County Technical School was one of many boons she made possible for the Guntersville area. Sadly, Lurleen succumbed to cancer on May 7, 1968. In honor of the first lady turned governor, the City of Guntersville eventually dubbed a street Lurleen B. Wallace Drive.

George Wallace (right) promised Jay Gurley that the State Publicity Bureau would help to advertise Cathedral Caverns. He professed to have enjoyed his time in Marshall County and described the cave as stupendous, "really colossal." While he had heard a great deal about the site, he had never previously visited the attraction.

Jay Gurley provided George Wallace a personal, private tour of the caverns. In his speech, Wallace said, "I've been telling about Cathedral Caverns in newspaper interviews and in making film clips but it's all what was told to me. Now I know firsthand what they've been telling me is true. I've been in caverns in other parts of the country and I know that none of them exceeds this one."

While appreciating the splendor of the cave, George Wallace (right) listened intently to Jay Gurley's plans for the site. Wallace continued, "Jay Gurley is an inspiring person to be around and he and Mrs. Gurley have done a tremendous job in developing Cathedral Caverns. We hope to do even more in the future than in the past to publicize this great scenic wonder."

In order to further thank George Wallace for his support of Alabama tourism, Jay Gurley gave him $224 in pennies from the Cathedral Caverns wishing well to donate to the charity of his choice. Wallace was very moved by this gesture and assured the audience of his continued dedication to advertising the state.

George Wallace decided to give the 160 pounds of coins, about two years' worth, to the United Givers Fund (UGF). He asked if any of the 350 people present was affiliated with the organization, but no one spoke. Wallace jokingly added, "Of course, if the UGF doesn't want it, I can use it in my next campaign."

George Wallace granted Jay Gurley permission to use his photographs in an array of advertisements for the cave. This image appeared in local newspapers like the *Advertiser-Gleam*. Its caption read, "Governor George Wallace invites you to visit Cathedral Caverns." Wallace was extremely popular in the area, and Gurley felt his support would bolster business.

Two days after the dinner, George Wallace wrote a letter to Jay Gurley. In it, he says, "I cannot tell you how much I enjoyed my visit to Grant and Cathedral Caverns. . . . It was certainly a fine experience for me. I was delighted to have an opportunity to tour the caverns at last and I find them to be everything you have said and more."

Jay Gurley was an imaginative promoter. He bought a van and fitted it with a microphone and speakers. During events like the Guntersville Boat Races (below), he would drive around announcing, "It's hot out here, but it's cool in Cathedral Caverns." He also drove through campgrounds, swimming areas, and other gathering places. (Courtesy of Jerry W. Cornelius Collection, Guntersville Historical Society.)

In the late 1960s, Cathedral Caverns' fame continued to rise, and it was designated a Cold War fallout shelter by the US Office of Civil Defense. Government officials expected that the cave could hold 10,000 people. In case of calamity, they ordered the stockpiling of things like food, medical necessities, and water-filtering products inside the cave. (Author's collection.)

The Gurley children attended Kate Duncan Smith DAR School in Grant (depicted here). Growing up during the Cold War, Robin Gurley often worried about how to get her friends to the cave if something catastrophic happened. In her words, "Those were serious times, but I was confident we would survive because we would be in the cave." (Courtesy of Jerry W. Cornelius Collection, Guntersville Historical Society.)

Shown is Nancy Gross, Marshall County High School's "Sweetheart of '63." Jay Gurley received a $60,000 business loan in 1966. In 1968, he finished the picnic area, expanded the parking lot, and created an attractive rock garden. He also revved up his publicity campaign with an advertisement containing the following: "Cathedral Caverns, Primitive Splendor within the Heart of Dixie." (Courtesy of Barbara Snow.)

One advertisement read, "Come to Cathedral Caverns! A warm welcome awaits you here at Cathedral Caverns. It's always a thrill to greet our visitors as it is only a comparatively short time ago when this fabulous cavern was hidden, unknown and beyond roadways. Here, deep within 'The Heart of Dixie,' you will truly be awed and inspired." (Courtesy of Guntersville Museum.)

Thirteen lieutenants from Rangoon, Burma, toured the cave on June 22, 1958. They had been studying at Anniston's Fort McClellan. In one Cathedral Caverns publication, Jay Gurley said, "Many of these visitors have told of the caverns in their countries, but agree that none can compare with Cathedral Caverns." (Courtesy of Cathedral Caverns State Park.)

A 1968 Cathedral Caverns advertisement includes this photograph of a picnic area that could sit 200. The caption reads, "Ample, clean picnic tables under shelter make Cathedral Caverns an ideal place for family outings. While mother and dad linger over a second cup of coffee, the children can enjoy wandering through the nature sculptured rock garden." (Courtesy of Cathedral Caverns State Park.)

The second Cathedral Caverns Welcome Center had 8,000 square feet and included a souvenir shop, a restaurant, an office, storage space, and restrooms. The base was made of old chimney stones that Jay Gurley had either bought or been given. Gurley also used 11,000 concrete blocks and "two and a half tons of tinted glass." (Courtesy of Cathedral Caverns State Park.)

The new welcome center can be seen in the background. Jay Gurley's love for Cathedral Caverns increased with time. He later reflected, "It's a wonder like the Grand Canyon or the Petrified Forest. Everyone should see it. I wanted everybody in the world to see it." On his first glimpse of Bat Cave, Gurley said, "I haven't been the same since." (Courtesy of Betty McGowin Jones.)

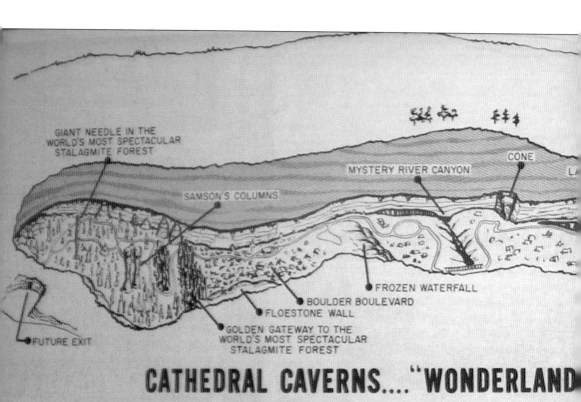

GIANT NEEDLE IN THE WORLD'S MOST SPECTACULAR STALAGMITE FOREST

SAMSON'S COLUMNS

MYSTERY RIVER CANYON

CONE

FROZEN WATERFALL

BOULDER BOULEVARD

FLOESTONE WALL

GOLDEN GATEWAY TO THE WORLD'S MOST SPECTACULAR STALAGMITE FOREST

FUTURE EXIT

CATHEDRAL CAVERNS...."WONDERLAND

A map published by Cathedral Caverns, Inc., in 1968 shows the vast interior of the cave. Jay Gurley called the cave "Wonderland Underland." He was stunned that it had gone relatively unnoticed before he purchased it. In Jules Verne's *Journey to the Center of the Earth*, one character, Prof. Otto Liedenbrock, states that he is far more interested in what lies below rather than on the surface. This thought was shared by Gurley, who always saw the cave as a special world apart. A

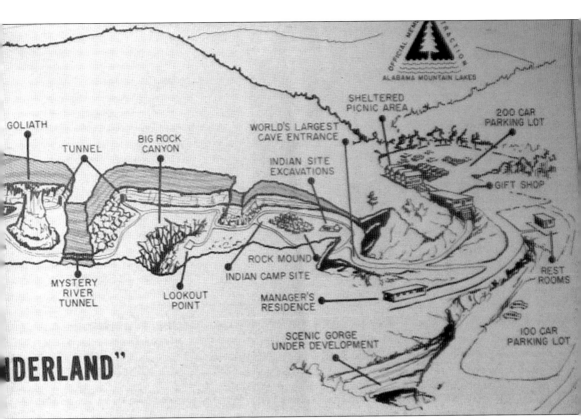

GOLIATH

TUNNEL

BIG ROCK CANYON

WORLD'S LARGEST CAVE ENTRANCE

INDIAN SITE EXCAVATIONS

SHELTERED PICNIC AREA

ALABAMA MOUNTAIN LAKES

200 CAR PARKING LOT

GIFT SHOP

ROCK MOUND INDIAN CAMP SITE

MYSTERY RIVER TUNNEL

LOOKOUT POINT

MANAGER'S RESIDENCE

REST ROOMS

SCENIC GORGE UNDER DEVELOPMENT

100 CAR PARKING LOT

IDERLAND"

man with a vision, he took a leap of faith and successfully transformed an undeveloped cave into an internationally known tourist attraction. By this time, the caverns had been open less than 20 years but already had widespread support not only in and around Marshall County but also throughout the state of Alabama. (Courtesy of Cathedral Caverns State Park.)

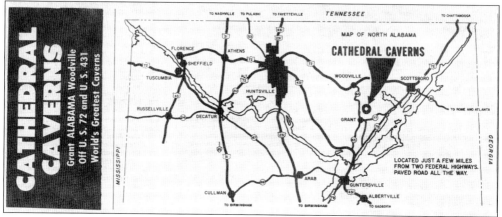

A map indicates the location of Cathedral Caverns in proximity to many northern Alabama cities. The distances in miles from Cathedral Caverns to the mentioned cities are as follows: Albertville (29); Arab (32); Athens (64); Birmingham (90); Cullman (57); Decatur (55); Florence (104); Guntersville (18); Huntsville (31); Russellville (103); Scottsboro (23); and Tuscumbia (99). Of significance, Cathedral Caverns was never segregated. (Courtesy of Betty McGowin Jones.)

A car enthusiast, Jay Gurley often allowed friends to take their cars into the cave, but this ploy was mainly to help advertising. The very fact that vehicles could travel to a certain point in the cave was pretty impressive. Driving into the cave was most likely a riveting but enjoyable feeling.

While called the "Frozen Waterfall," this was really a flowstone structure measuring 100 by 30 feet that appeared to have been carved by running water. For effect, Jay Gurley pumped water over the rocks to give the impression of a waterfall. Today, this feature continues to be a favorite of tourists. (Courtesy of Betty McGowin Jones.)

This image depicts a girl posing atop the Columned Tower. In September 1971, Jay Gurley said, "If this were the west or any place besides Alabama, this would be a national park." He argued that Cathedral Caverns outshone rivals like Carlsbad Caverns National Park and Mammoth Cave National Park. In his words, "Many caves do not have beautiful sights and colors like we do." (Courtesy of Cheryl Kennamer.)

Cathedral Caverns, Ala.

Shown are Rhonda Troup and Ray Selvage. When asked what made Cathedral Caverns exceptional, Jay Gurley said, "Others [cave tourist attractions] used colored lights to create an effect. All we use light for is to guide the way, and we are trying to hide them. Nothing seen in a cave should be man-made. That destroys the purpose of it." (Courtesy of Guntersville Museum.)

Scottsboro High School students are shown clowning around in their Stone Age attire. Kenneth Gurley became the new manager of Cathedral Caverns in late 1971 and remained in that position for two years. Jay Gurley said, "I'm worn out, mentally and physically. You don't know how relieved I am to turn the management over to a man I know will do a good job."

Ray Selvage and Rhonda Troup (in front) pose with Sammy McBride and Robin Gurley in the Golden Gateway. An Air Force veteran, Kenneth Gurley moved his family from Michigan and relocated near the cave. Upon taking the position as manager, Gurley said, "Much of the experience I have gained should help to establish Cathedral Caverns as one of the truly magnificent natural landmarks in the United States." (Courtesy of Guntersville Museum.)

While Kenneth Gurley's presence alleviated some stress, Jay Gurley, ever the workaholic, busied himself with a slew of projects like forming a campground and upgrading the concession stand. To help with these remodeling tasks, he applied for and received a $125,000 loan from the US Small Business Administration. (Courtesy of Guntersville Museum.)

Jackie Hodges is perched atop a formation. In July 1972, Cathedral Caverns gained its first female guide, Jo Ann Hodgens, a Grant native and a sophomore at Jacksonville State University. To cut expenses, the Gurleys decided the cave would no longer be open year-round. Instead, the open season would start on June 1 and end on Labor Day.

Jay Gurley believed the drop in patronage derived partly from local road construction, which lasted much longer than expected. Because nearby Guntersville Caverns had recently closed, he probably feared a decline in tourism in general. Operating expenses exceeded income, and this financial shortfall proved immensely worrisome for the family. (Courtesy of Guntersville Museum.)

In an interview with the *Advertiser-Gleam*, Jay Gurley says, "I still think it could be a national park if we could just get enough public and political support behind it." In 1972, US senators John Sparkman (D-AL, shown) and James Allen (D-AL) introduced a bill to make Cathedral Caverns a national monument. They both believed it to be a natural treasure worthy of federal recognition. (Courtesy of Guntersville Museum.)

In June 1972, a 30-member youth orchestra performed in Cathedral Caverns. Instead of an event open to the public, it was an experiment with sound. The participants wanted to experience how music echoed in the cave. In the words of Kenneth Gurley, "When's the last time you heard Mendelssohn 250 feet underground?" (Courtesy of *Advertiser-Gleam*.)

Rosemary Champion, Guntersville's Carlisle Park Middle School band director, played a flute solo during this concert. From an array of nearby cities, the other musicians were attending a string workshop at a nearby camp. Directed by Livingston Gearhart of Buffalo, New York, the orchestra belted melodious sounds that, due to the overwhelming echo, almost deafened all concerned. (Courtesy of *Advertiser-Gleam*.)

Alabama lieutenant governor Jere Beasley received a tour of Cathedral Caverns in June 1972. This was in recognition of the cave's being designated "one of the six most outstanding caverns in America" by the US Travel Service. During the visit, Beasley stated his belief that the cave should become a national park. (Courtesy of *Advertiser-Gleam*.)

A group of Scottsboro High School girls is shown in Cathedral Caverns. The other five "outstanding caverns" were Carlsbad Caverns, Mammoth Cave, Luray Caverns, Wind Cave, and Mark Twain Cave. Then director of the Alabama Mountain Lakes Association Grace Dees said, "These six will be used in all Visit USA exhibits, seminars and campaigns throughout the foreign market area."

This advertisement shows the proximity of Huntsville, "Outer Space Capital," to Cathedral Caverns, "Inner Space Capital." Jay Gurley spent years collecting antiques like church bells. Plans for a frontier village also included a store, gristmill, sorghum mill, and blacksmith shop. Rather than raise admission prices to fund the project, Gurley eventually scrapped the idea. The artifacts were auctioned on May 6, 1972. (Courtesy of Marshall County Archives.)

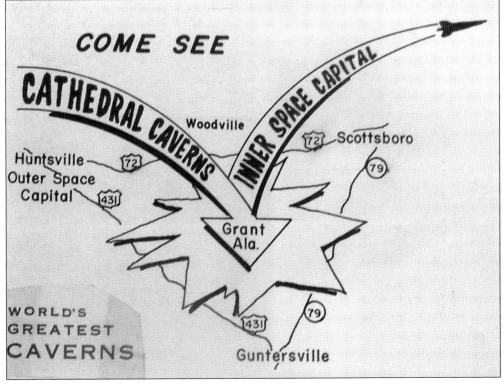

The original Cathedral Caverns Welcome Center sold souvenir plates. Jay Gurley loved automobiles and could often be seen driving around and even inside the cave. His specialty was driving backwards. As Robin Gurley reflected, "He'd go flying it seems like. Flying down that road and these people, especially the women would be screaming. And I'd be in the back going, oh, this is no big deal." (Author's collection.)

This is a vintage ashtray once sold by Cathedral Caverns. Toys went quickly and were often priced at approximately a dollar. Many boys, however, preferred to buy green cigars with a Cathedral Caverns label. Visitors, young and old, often purchased at least one memento. Those who still own objects bought at the pre-park Cathedral Caverns cherish them as keepsakes. (Author's collection.)

This is a vintage teacup once sold at Cathedral Caverns. In the late 1950s, it was purchased by Guntersville native Barbara Snow. Though only 14 at the time, she vividly remembers the experience. Her parents, Kenneth and Cora Gross, had heard a great deal about the cave and wanted to see it for themselves. Kenneth, especially, was enthralled by the geological formations and the gigantic interior. (Author's collection.)

These are toys once sold at Cathedral Caverns. In September 1973, Donald Windsor, a botany technician from the University of Florida, bicycled 620 miles to Cathedral Caverns. He heard about it from his landlord, Connie Mae Kirkland, a former Marshall County resident. Windsor said, "I've seen several of the better known caves, but this one has got to be the best one yet." (Courtesy of Cheryl Kennamer.)

Jay Gurley believed the cave's location deterred the federal government from making it a national park. He said, "There are no national parks of this type in the South. They probably would take it over if I gave it to them. But I can't do that. I've sacrificed my family for this. I've gone into debt. I wasn't even able to send my kids to college." (Courtesy of Guntersville Museum.)

Cathedral Caverns became a registered National Natural Landmark in 1972. With Jay Gurley (left) is Dr. William Hendricksen, the Department of the Interior Southeast Region's assistant director for professional services. To commemorate the occasion, Gurley was given a certificate and a bronze plaque. A bittersweet victory, this event proved an honor and validation for Gurley but did not soothe the cave's mounting financial difficulties.

Shown chatting at the dedication are, from left to right, Dr. William Hendricksen, Jay Gurley, Helen Gurley, and US representative Tom Bevill (D-AL). Bevill, who believed Cathedral Caverns was of immeasurable value to the state, had been seeking this classification for years. Cathedral Caverns became one of 140 National Natural Landmarks in the United States at the time and one of a handful in Alabama. While thrilled that the cave became a natural landmark, Jay was nevertheless preoccupied with debt. The irony of the ill-timed tribute was not lost on him. He and Helen ventured to hope that this designation might spark federal interest in making the cave a national park. This distinction is something that Jay in particular had always desired. He believed it would validate his life's work. (Courtesy of University Libraries Division of Special Collections, the University of Alabama.)

Jay Gurley (right) had the support of numerous Alabama politicians like US representative Tom Bevill. Ever since Gurley purchased the cave, politician had lent both willing ears and hands. They knew the caverns attracted tourists from across the globe, who brought in much-needed dollars to the local and state economies.

From left to right, Kenneth Gurley, Rep. Tom Bevill, and Jay Gurley are seen standing in front of the cave entrance. Bevill, who served in Congress between 1967 and 1997, represented Alabama's Fourth and later Seventh Districts. According to Brett J. Derbes, managing editor of the Texas State Historical Association, "He [Bevill] became known as 'The King of Pork' for securing federal money for development projects in his district."

Rep. Tom Bevill is shown giving a speech in Guntersville. He was a fan of the state parks, especially the ones in his district. Lake Guntersville State Park has Tom Bevill Trail, which is roughly three miles. The formation of Little River Canyon National Preserve in Cherokee County was in part due to the actions of Bevill. (Courtesy of *Advertiser-Gleam*.)

Kenneth Gurley (left) is shown talking to Rep. Tom Bevill. When roadside construction inflicted massive damage to tourist numbers, Jay and Helen Gurley found themselves unable to repay a loan. Overwhelmed, they did something they never thought possible—they sold the property. Doing so was like severing a part of their souls.

Jay Gurley poses for a photograph with his daughter Kathleen. Jay later reflected, "Without traffic flow, there was no income. I could have weathered it for 1½ years, but not 3½ years. It was the worst of times. I couldn't do anything." Guntersville contractor Dave Du'Chemin, formerly of Sandborn, Indiana, bought a controlling interest. With the swipe of a pen, on March 17, 1974, an era ended. Gurley immediately regretted selling and could only watch as the caverns he loved went through an uncertain period. While this proved an unfortunate end to the Gurley era, Jay knew he and his family had achieved something phenomenal during their tenure at the cave. All the adventures, interactions, sights, and sensations had been exceptional, and moreover, he had the satisfaction of knowing that the caverns would continue to awe.

Three

Transition of Ownership and Formation of Cathedral Caverns State Park

Dave Du'Chemin (right), shown with Jay and Helen Gurley, had an array of promotions in mind. Announcing that the cave would be open year-round except for Thanksgiving and Christmas, he planned to extend the tour path and add a tour of Lake Guntersville. Du'Chemin hoped to refashion the cave as "Country Town USA," an Opryland-type attraction that would host musicians and concerts. (Courtesy of Jerry Cornelius Collection, Guntersville Historical Society.)

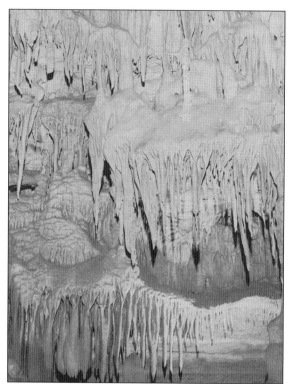

In April 1974, Dave Du'Chemin had an old World War I boxcar brought to a road near the cave. The boxcar, built in France in 1898, had previously been in Montgomery, Birmingham, and Huntsville. Deeming it eye-catching, he used the boxcar as a large sign with which to lure drivers onto Cathedral Caverns Highway, the route leading from the main road. (Courtesy of *Advertiser-Gleam*.)

In a discussion with representatives from the Hank Williams Memorial Commission, Dave Du'Chemin made arrangements for the cave to host the Hank Williams Salute. Sixteen singers ranging from Hank Williams Jr. to Freddie Hart were lined up. Due primarily to expense, the salute was postponed from September 13–15, 1974, to June 27–29, 1975, but in the end it never occurred. (Courtesy of *Advertiser-Gleam*.)

This is an aerial view of Lake Guntersville. Named Sonny and Cher, two 3-year-old lions struck Dave Du'Chemin as being a noteworthy addition to the Cathedral Caverns family and, maybe, the beginnings of a zoo. The siblings, who arrived at the cave site in March 1975, had been raised from the age of five months by Bobby Cannon, who had recently closed Cannon's Nature Land in Huntsville. (Courtesy of *Advertiser-Gleam*.)

Bobby Cannon, who referred to Sonny and Cher as "babies," volunteered to check on them once a day. The lions were placed in a temporary, makeshift pen near the machine shop, but a larger sanctuary was later built near the cave entrance. Their presence resulted in a temporary surge of tourists. (Courtesy of *Advertiser-Gleam*.)

In addition to the lions, Dave Du'Chemin started a publicity stunt he dubbed a "cave-in." Customers could pay for the chance to spend the night in Cathedral Caverns. For a small sum, they received a night tour, slept in the cave, and were served breakfast the next morning. This gimmick worked best with teenagers and diehard cave buffs. (Courtesy of *Advertiser-Gleam*.)

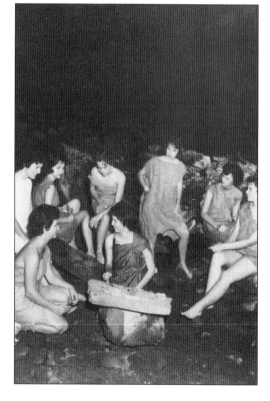

These Scottsboro High School students had fun during this photo session. Due to financial problems, Dave Du'Chemin closed Cathedral Caverns in the late summer of 1975. During this time, Cathedral Caverns was plugged by the syndicated comic strip *Fun Facts by Wrigley's Spearmint Gum*: "World's largest stalagmite is 60 feet tall and 200 feet around. Named Goliath, it's in Cathedral Caverns near Grant, Alabama."

An unidentified Scottsboro High School students stands on a rock formation while having her photograph taken. Shortly after Dave Du'Chemin closed the cave, Bill Grafton became president of Cathedral Caverns, Inc. On August 2, 1977, Tom German, a Huntsville fabric shop owner, bought the cave at auction for $325,000. This sum did not cover the property's debt, some $422,000 plus bankruptcy court expenses. Even so, German had faced competition.

The bidding started at $100,000. The top bidders were Tom German, Mario Bottesini, president of the Bank of Huntsville; Bud Keetch of Dallas, Texas; and the People's State Bank of Grant. Upon winning the auction, German was interviewed by the *Advertiser-Gleam* and purportedly confessed, "I don't much like caves." (Courtesy of Guntersville Museum.)

Tom German had never been to Cathedral Caverns until the day of the auction. Having heard about the sale at the last minute, he attended on an impulse and bought the cave sight unseen. With two fabric shops and other real estate investments, German had business experience and wanted to reopen within a year.

A young Kenneth Gurley poses for a photograph in the Stalagmite Forest. Tom German said, "I think it may be worth more than what I paid for it. It's in the center of the recreation facilities of North Alabama, right between Huntsville, Goose Pond, and Scottsboro, and the State Park at Guntersville. Highways [US 72 and US 431] will be going past it in both directions. I feel like I made a good investment."

In the fall of 1980, German leased Cathedral Caverns to Bluegrass Hoppers, Inc., a group of nine Scottsboro businessmen led by John Franklin. These men renamed the cave Cathedral Caverns Bluegrass Park and opened it on November 8, 1980. Perhaps seeking a reputation similar to that of Opryland, they invited many bluegrass performers to appear. Dan Kirtland managed the park. (Courtesy of Guntersville Museum.)

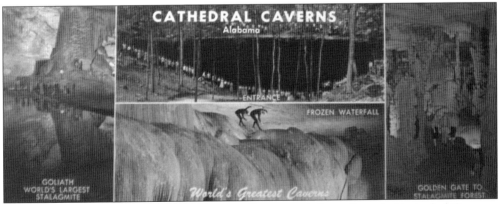

On July 4, 1982, Bill Monroe of the Bluegrass Boys recorded an album in Cathedral Caverns. Due to technical, sound-related issues, Monroe failed to release the songs he recorded there. They have since been sold in the boxed set *Bill Monroe: My Last Days on Earth*. In addition to hosting musicians, the Bluegrass Hoppers also planned to add a campground. (Courtesy of Betty McGowin Jones.)

These are two of the Scottsboro High School students once photographed as cave people. In summer 1983, the movie *Secrets of the Phantom Caverns* (aka *What Waits Below*), starring Timothy Bottoms, Lisa Blount, A.C. Weary, and Robert Powell, was filmed at Cathedral Caverns. Powell's wife, Babs, and Weary's wife, Kim Zimmer, who played Echo Disavoy on *One Life to Live*, visited the area.

Based on a story by Ken Barnett, the plot involves a group of American officers stationed in Belize. Ordered to place sonic testers in nearby caverns, two men enter and discover an unknown people, the Lemurians, who have ultraviolet vision, sonar speech, and exceptional hearing. The makeup artist for the film was Bill Munns, famous for *Swamp Thing*. Pictured here is Jackie Hodges. (Courtesy of Betty McGowin Jones.)

Filming began at Cathedral Caverns on August 8 and finished at Cumberland Caverns at McMinnville, Tennessee. Many Marshall County locals volunteered to be extras. Directed by Don Sharp, the movie was partially produced by Robert Bailey, known for *Superman* and *Star Trek: The Motion Picture*. Pictured here is Walter Wright. (Courtesy of Guntersville Museum.)

Cathedral Caverns, Ala

During filming, 13 cast members had to be hospitalized due to carbon monoxide emissions from the gas generator powering the cave's lights. The movie failed at the box office, but most extras expressed no regret. Tour guide Dale Kells stated, "The entire experience was one of the best times of my teenage life. I would do it all again, noxious gas and all." This is another humorous Stone Age take.

In March 1987, an array of local and state politicians toured Cathedral Caverns. Pictured are, from left to right, Rep. Ben Richardson (Scottsboro), Rep. Euclid Rains (Albertville), Jackson County commissioner Gene Wells, Sen. Lowell Barron (Fyffe), Mayor Bob Hembree (Guntersville), state conservation commissioner James Martin, Sen. Ann Bedsole (Mobile), Sen. Loyd Coleman (Arab), Rep. Gordon Ray Moon (Guntersville), Jay Gurley, Mayor Haden Chandler (Grant), Tom German's representative Bert Danner (Huntsville), and Matthew Danner. (Courtesy of *Advertiser-Gleam*.)

In 1985, state senator Hinton Mitchem (D-Albertville) (pictured) and state senator Loyd Coleman (D-Arab) managed to persuade the state legislature to allocate $750,000 for Cathedral Caverns. Expense concerns in the legislature coupled with the initial asking price of Tom German delayed the sale, but the State of Alabama purchased the cave and 461 acres for $500,000 in July 1987. (Courtesy of *Advertiser-Gleam*.)

Pictured are, from left to right, 1959 Marshall County High School juniors Carl Wisener, Angel Wisener, Sandra Johnson, and Linda Word. Jay Gurley had frequently toured other commercial caves like those in Branson, Missouri. All the while, he spoke with owners or officials and exchanged ideas about tourism. Ideally, he had dreamed of Cathedral Caverns becoming a national park, but he was ecstatic when it became a state park. (Courtesy of Barbara Snow.)

Around June 1990, signs like this were erected. Even though Cathedral Caverns had been closed, its fame meant that tourists, some from great distances, kept coming. When they arrived, frustration and confusion ensued. The sign may have deterred locals, but since the cave still appeared in various advertisements throughout the country, people mistakenly believed it to be open for business. (Courtesy of *Advertiser-Gleam*.)

After buying the cave, the State of Alabama initiated a series of improvements that delayed reopening for 13 years. When he retired in 2011, state senator Hinton Mitchem said, "I got a lot of criticism for Cathedral Caverns. The papers in Montgomery said I was throwing money down the biggest hole in the world for nothing. But it's the best thing I've done. That will be my legacy."

Scottsboro High School students pretend to cook over a fire in the cave. On June 22, 1993, Alabama first lady Marsha Folsom, wife of Gov. Jim Folsom Jr., visited the cave and announced that funding, a federal grant of $880,000, had been secured to expedite the park's opening. She remarked, "My parents brought me to this wonderful place when I was a child. It is something I will never forget."

The Great Wall of China Miniature is located in the Crystal Room. Between March and December 1993, the Huntsville Grotto National Speleological Society mapped the caverns. Its report suggests that the state limit visitors to the Crystal Room, a small cave with two chambers of white, shining walls of calcite, located far beyond the tour walkway. (Courtesy of Cathedral Caverns State Park.)

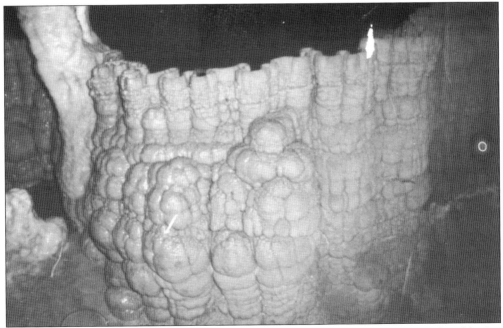

This miniature is an arresting sight. The Crystal Room had originally been explored by Jay Gurley. Few save spelunkers had been permitted access. To enter, people had to squeeze their bodies through a narrow opening. Although arduous, the trouble was well worth the enchanting sights within this chamber. (Courtesy of Cathedral Caverns State Park.)

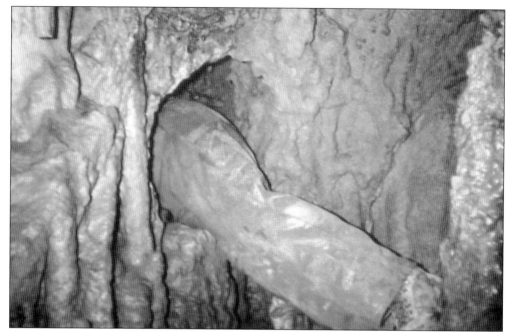

A man could enter the Crystal Room through the 18-inch opening. Once in the hole, he would have to crawl about 10 feet before reaching the room. Full of stalactites and stalagmites, the chamber is almost like a winter wonderland because many of its formations look like they are covered in either frost or snow. (Courtesy of Cathedral Caverns State Park.)

Beyond the normal public tour, the Crystal Room is rather difficult to access. In addition to the awkward position of the entrance tunnel, it and the room itself are rather cramped. Visitors have damaged this chamber by breaking off pieces of the mineral deposits for souvenirs. The Crystal Room is currently off-limits. (Courtesy of Cathedral Caverns State Park.)

John Neely (of Foley) and Mary Dobbs (of Decatur) are shown at Huntsville's premiere of *Tom & Huck*, a movie partly filmed at Cathedral Caverns. During shooting there, between April and June 1995, locals served as extras. With teen heartthrob Jonathan Taylor Thomas in town, many area girls flocked to Grant to get a glimpse. (© *Huntsville Times*, 1995. All rights reserved. Used with permission of Alabama Media Group.)

One extra, a Mrs. Sisk, reflected, "What overwhelmed me most was the natural beauty of Alabama. The caves, the Tennessee River, the greenery, the mountain laurel. I'm so proud to be an Alabamian." The *Huntsville Times* speculated that the movie had brought the area $2 million in tourism. (Courtesy of Guntersville Museum.)

Jay Gurley, still grieving for his wife, who had passed away in 1986, took some solace in the park, the fruits of their shared labor. He still lived near the cave and gladly accepted the state's offer for him to act as both consultant and caretaker. He looked forward to running a gift shop and museum.

Jay Gurley's license plate read "1 CVMN." In one of his last interviews, he said, "It's [Cathedral Caverns] a wonder like the Grand Canyon. . . . Everyone should see it. It had become my life. When you dedicate your life to something 24 hours a day, seven days a week, for more than 20 years, it becomes so much a part of you that you can't drop it."

State conservation commissioner Jim Martin (pointing) and state representative Howard Hawk (D-Arab) (right) speak with visitors at the cave site. In May 1996, US senator Richard Shelby (R-AL) paid a visit to Cathedral Caverns and met with Martin and Jay Gurley. The meeting occurred one week before Gurley's death. (Courtesy of *Advertiser-Gleam*.)

This is one of the last photographs taken of Jay Gurley. Long plagued by heart trouble, his health had deteriorated to the extent that he no longer dared enter his beloved cave alone. On April 30, 1996, he died in Huntsville Hospital after suffering another heart attack. His memorial service took place at Lane Chapel at Grant's DAR School. Those in attendance mourned the man but celebrated the life.

Friends, family, and former employees met that evening in the DAR School's Home Economics Department meeting room to look at old photographs, reminisce, and recall the adventures of the Gurley era at Cathedral Caverns. They took comfort in the fact that Jay Gurley's dream for the cave was coming true. That same year, Cathedral Caverns gained a park ranger, Danny Lewis (pictured). (Courtesy of Cathedral Caverns State Park.)

Jacksonville State University professor Dr. Danny Vaughn (pictured) studied Cathedral Caverns in the summer of 1988. At a ground-breaking ceremony for a new trail in 1997, Gov. Fob James, a former Auburn running back, noted the cave's opening could hold a football field. James said, "I've heard about it all my life and have never been here before. I was just amazed when I saw the breadth of the entrance." (Courtesy of Advertiser-Gleam.)

This image features Gov. Fob James. In a conversation with *Advertiser-Gleam* reporter Anthony Campbell, James said, "My punts were always straight up and didn't have a lot of distance. I understand it's over 100 feet from the floor to the ceiling here [Cathedral Caverns]. That's tall enough." (Courtesy of *Advertiser-Gleam*.)

This is a headshot of state representative Frank McDaniel (D-Albertville). McDaniel, who eventually served five terms in office before retiring in 2010, was an ardent supporter of Cathedral Caverns. While in office, he served on the County and Municipal Government Committee and as chair of the Commerce Committee. (Courtesy of *Advertiser-Gleam*.)

Robin Gurley and an unidentified model are shown posing for a postcard. While three of the four Gurley children had moved away, Robin still lived in Marshall County. She, like her siblings, devoured any news about the cave and anxiously observed its gradual transformation into a state park.

These are unidentified Marshall County High School athletes in 1959. State representative Howard Hawk, state senator Hinton Mitchem, state conservation commissioner Jim Martin, contractor Tony Christopher, Gov. Fob James, and state representative Frank McDaniel participated in a ground-breaking for a trail at Cathedral Caverns. A minister said, "This is a first for me . . . I've never blessed a hole in the ground before." (Courtesy of Barbara Snow.)

To further emphasize the cave's history, state conservation commissioner Jim Martin believed a Native American diorama would boost tourism. Plans for a campground with four adults, a boy, a girl, and a baby were prepared. The background was to include a deer being cured and a rabbit being cooked over a fire. A state legislature contract review committee deemed the estimated cost of $242,000 too expensive, so it was never completed. (Courtesy of *Advertiser-Gleam*.)

Guntersville locals are shown playing music. They are, from left to right, unidentified (saxophone), Jerry Glenn Vaughn (trombone), James Corpeling (piano); and Bill Hill (bass). The State of Alabama spent roughly $400,000 to construct a bridge across the gorge in Cathedral Caverns. So as to build from scratch, it also tore down all existing buildings on the property. (Courtesy of Marshall County Archives.)

Scottsboro High School girls pose with a fake dinosaur. During the fall of 1997, a two-mile road connecting the cave to the highway was under construction. The Marshall County Convention and Visitors Bureau worked with the Alabama Bureau of Tourism to promote the new park. At long last, on May 5, 2000, Cathedral Caverns State Park held an open house attended by Gov. Don Siegelman and a crowd of 2,500.

Upon setting eyes on Goliath, Gov. Don Siegelman (pictured) said, "Ooh, wow." On Cathedral Caverns in general, he remarked, "This is a natural landmark. It's a natural wonder of the world. This will quickly become a place the people of Alabama will want to come and see. We have to make sure the world knows it's here." (Courtesy of *Advertiser-Gleam*.)

This is a vintage postcard advertising Guntersville's old Val Monte Motel, which opened in 1958. It was a high-end tourist resort that sported a pool and the city's first golf course. Over the years, many celebrities, ranging from Western movie star Lash LaRue to television child actor Jeremy Gelbwaks (of *Partridge Family* fame), stayed there. (Courtesy of Marshall County Archives.)

Shown is Ray Selvage. Members of the Guntersville Chamber of Commerce had anxiously awaited the park's opening. Its president, Luanne Hayes, expected Cathedral Caverns State Park might persuade tourists to stay an extra day when visiting Lake Guntersville State Park. At the time, Guntersville Airport's World War I Replica Fighter Museum had closed, so the city needed another attraction. (Courtesy of Guntersville Museum.)

115

Cathedral Caverns is featured in the Winter 1996 issue of *Outdoor Alabama*. An article titled "Dreams Come True—Eventually" describes the state's initial purchase of the cave and the plans to make it a state park. Alabama State Parks director Gary Leach is quoted as saying, "We hope that all Alabamians—and indeed all Americans—will come enjoy this unique natural wonder." (Courtesy of *Advertiser-Gleam*.)

Judy Gurley and DAR School teacher Jimmy Stanton pose on the Frozen Waterfall. On December 2, 2003, a party heralding the new welcome center was attended by Gov. Bob Riley. Riley said, "Cathedral Caverns personifies the diversity of Alabama." The park has been mentioned in magazines ranging from *Southern Living* to *National Geographic*.

This is a view from Grant Mountain. In April 2005, Danny Lewis became the park's manager. He had served as a park ranger at both Cathedral Caverns State Park and Lake Guntersville State Park. Lewis said, "There's no way you can put down in words how beautiful this place really is." He added, "I'll never be the same knowing the man [Jay Gurley]. He made a tremendous impact on my life." (Author's collection.)

Cathedral Caverns State Park frequently receives letters of inquiry. In March 2006, Miroslav Dubravay of the Czech Republic wrote, "Please send me some postcards of your cave." In April 2006, Norma Hartman, a first-grade teacher at Scott Elementary School in Evansville, Indiana, had her students write for information on the cave. (Courtesy of *Advertiser-Gleam*.)

Floestone Wall

Visitors often send thank-you notes. Carol Hursh of Kansas City, Missouri, wrote, "You made my day." John Grooms of Des Plaines, Illinois, wrote, "Since we have been home we have raved about the beauty of your caverns, how accommodating you were, the history, the humor, and world records." Dorothy Douglas of Cottondale, Florida, wrote, "They are the greatest caverns we have been in." (Courtesy of Cheryl Kennamer.)

Danny Lewis once said, "If a man loves what he does, he never works a day in his life," a belief Jay Gurley had exemplified. After Lewis resigned in December 2008, Lamar Pendergrass (left) became park superintendent and remains in that position to this day. Also pictured is tour guide Alex Prickett. (Courtesy of Lamar Pendergrass.)

Lamar Pendergrass had previously worked as the assistant park superintendent at DeSoto State Park in DeKalb County, Alabama. He currently manages both Cathedral Caverns State Park and Rickwood Caverns State Park in Warrior, Alabama. Pendergrass has been quoted as follows: "This [Cathedral Caverns] is a popular place. . . . We're not too far from Lake Guntersville and DeSoto, so sometimes people may come here, then go to another park."

This is the Cathedral Caverns State Park Welcome Center. It sells items like T-shirts, gemstones, baseball hats, postcards, stuffed animals, and books. Visitors can rest and enjoy the scenery in comfortable rocking chairs on the shaded verandas. In 2012, the park received a $9,625 grant from the National Park Service. The grant was used to install LED lights in the cave. (Author's collection.)

On April 16, 2014, Alabama first lady Dianne Bentley visited Cathedral Caverns as part of her "bucket list" to commemorate the 75th year of the state park system. Shown from left to right are Alabama state senator Clay Scofield, Bentley, Marshall County Tourism and Visitors Bureau president Katy Norton, and Lake Guntersville State Park superintendent Michael Jeffreys. (Courtesy of Judy Miller, Marshall County Legislative Office.)

Alabama first lady Dianne Bentley is pictured with Cathedral Caverns State Park superintendent Lamar Pendergrass. In his words, "Cathedral Caverns is a premier show cave in the United States." In 2014, the park received a Certificate of Excellence from TripAdvisor. (© *Huntsville Times*, 2014. All rights reserved. Used with permission of Alabama Media Group.)

Above is an information sign near the Cathedral Caverns State Park Welcome Center. It reads in part: "We offer a 1.3 mile walking tour of a world class show cave. The tour will last approximately 75–90 minutes. You will be walking along a smooth, concrete walkway with handrails, but we must caution that there are a number of areas with inclines/declines of about 45 degrees. The cave is stroller friendly for those of you with small children. The pathway is also wheelchair accessible, but we remind you again of the inclines/declines inside the cave. The temperature in the cave averages 58–61 degrees year round and there's no breeze." Below is a sign with information on tours and admissions. (Both, author's collection.)

Nestled in the mountains in a remote part of Marshall County, Cathedral Caverns is still isolated even today. There are beautiful vistas from the overlook in Grant. Nearby is the Kennamer Cove Trading Post, which is a popular setting for parties and weddings. It also has a great many vintage photographs on Kennamer Cove and Cathedral Caverns. (Author's collection.)

This is a sign with detailed information on the interior of Cathedral Caverns State Park. It provides the width and height of the various chambers as well as details about Mystery River, Stalagmite Mountain, Goliath, the Frozen Waterfall, Boulder Boulevard, the Flowstone Wall, and the Stalagmite Forest. (Author's collection.)

Children enjoy the Cathedral Caverns Mining Company, which offers gemstone and fossil panning. The instructions are as follows: "Select a bag of mining ore enriched with gems or fossils from around the world. Place part of the ore from the bag in a screen bottom box. Dip the box in the sluice and watch the gems appear as the soil washes away." (Author's collection.)

Lamar Pendergrass exhibited impressive ingenuity in acquiring this gem mine. Tourists often throw coins in the Cathedral Caverns well, so he collected some $6,000 in change to buy the mine. Salted bags can be purchased in the gift shop. To date, the mine has made $45,000 a year. (Author's collection.)

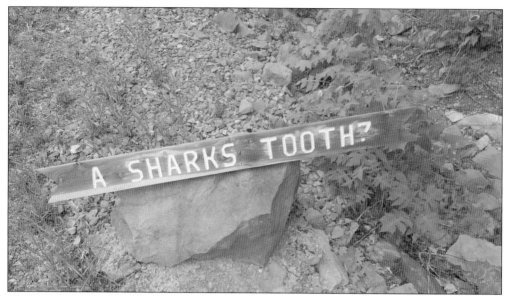

Eleven shark teeth have been found throughout Cathedral Caverns, which once lay at the bottom of a sea. Children are especially intrigued by the fact that sharks once swam the area. Because the teeth are often embedded in the cave's ceiling, tour guides shine a flashlight on them so tourists can see them with their own eyes. (Author's collection.)

These people are zealously trying to take pictures of a shark tooth in Cathedral Caverns. Tour guides will often point out fossils and various other features. Gazing at the formations is like cloud watching: One resembles a caveman holding a club. Another bears a striking similarity to the mask worn by Darth Vader. Yet another looks like Pres. Abraham Lincoln. (Courtesy of *Advertiser-Gleam*.)

Touring Cathedral Caverns State Park will certainly pique the senses. While walking from the parking lot to the visitor center, guests do not see the mouth of the cave until they round a corner. Astonishment is soon replaced by excitement, curiosity, and, for some, fear. And all of these feelings strike before the tour even begins. Just imagine what follows! (Author's collection.)

As tourists take their first steps into the cave, they often look back over their shoulders until the light fades away altogether. When they once more see the light on the return trek, many pick up their pace. Going from 60 degrees Fahrenheit to over 90 degrees in summers adds yet another dynamic to the Cathedral Caverns experience. (Author's collection.)

Grant native Alex Prickett, a tour guide at Cathedral Caverns State Park, is shown (center) with a group of Huntsville exchange students. Though Prickett has been in the cave more times than he can count, it never gets old. The responses of each tour mean that while the movie might have the same setting, the cast, lines, and scenes are constantly changing. (Courtesy of Alex Prickett.)

Cathedral Caverns State Park guides Shelby Ryan (left) and Trevor Darling (second from left) are shown as they embark on a tour. Each guide has his or her own style, but the basic story remains the same. Going on a tour is part adventure and part history lesson. The journey will leave guests with much food for thought about the cave and its impact on the area. (Author's collection.)